Waterproof
WESTERN AUSTRALIAN
FISH
GUIDE

by Frank Prokop

Illustrations by Trevor Hawkins
Rigs by Geoff Wilson

AMBERJACK

Scientific name: *Seriola dumerili.*

Description: A relatively large, fast swimming species mainly found in offshore waters in the vicinity of reefs or drop-offs. Sometimes confused with yellowtail kingfish, the amberjack has a dark blue to olive tail fin whereas the kingfish has a yellow tail fin. The anal fin of the amberjack is darker in colour with a characteristic white edging. Differs from similar samson fish in having more rays in the dorsal fin (32 – 33) versus 23 – 25 for the samson fish. The samson fish also appears to have red teeth, due to blood engorged gums.

The amberjack attains a weight of 36 kilograms.

Fishing: A hard fighting fish which takes feather or minnow lures trolled near reefs and drop offs. Amberjacks will also take both live and dead bait fished in the vicinity of offshore reefs.

The amberjack makes good eating, although larger specimens tend to be dry and coarse textured.

Rigs and Tactics:

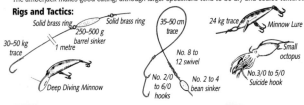

BASS, RED

Caution

POISONOUS

Scientific name: *Lutjanus bohar.*
Also known as Two spot red snapper, kelp bream, kelp sea perch.

Description: The red bass is a strikingly coloured fish which can be almost bright orange to a deep brick red. The scales have a paler centre which gives an attractive dappled effect. There is a diagnostic deep groove or channel (often described as a pit) which runs from the nostrils to the front of the eye. This groove distinguishes the red bass from the similar mangrove jack where larger specimens are also caught on offshore reefs. The snout is somewhat pointed. The tail fin is slightly indented and the ventral and anal fins may have a white margin. There is a moderate notch in the preopercular bone. Juvenile and sub-adult red bass have two or sometimes one silvery-white spots on the back, most prominent near the rear of the soft dorsal fin. The red bass can reach 13 kg and a length of 90 centimetres. Caution editing as a ciguatera risk even in WA.

BARRAMUNDI

Scientific name: *Lates calcarifer*. Also known as Barra, giant perch.

Description: The barramundi is a special fish which is as beautiful in reality as it is in the dreams of so many anglers. It has a small head with a large mouth and large eyes.

Barramundi have large scales and a particularly powerful tail. Coupled with their thick shoulders, barramundi can put up a good fight, many fish will exhibit the famous gill arching leaps when hooked.

The barramundi can be a brilliant silver colour for sea run fish, ranging to a very dark, chocolate brown colour for fish in billabongs at the end of the dry season or those grown in aquaculture facilities.

Small barra and those in aquaria exhibit a characteristic light stripe down the forehead between the eyes which becomes more pronounced when the fish is excited.

Barramundi in Australia change sex as they grow older (interestingly barramundi in Thailand do not change sex). All fish start out as males and, after spawning once or twice, become female for the rest of their lives. It is therefore impossible to catch a granddaddy barra as it would certainly be female. This sex change is more related to age than size, but barramundi over 8 kg are almost certainly all female.

Rigs and Tactics:

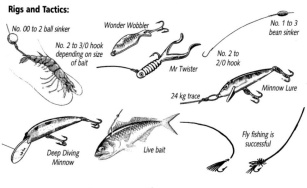

No. 00 to 2 ball sinker

Wonder Wobbler

No. 1 to 3 bean sinker

No. 2 to 3/0 hook depending on size of bait

Mr Twister

No. 2 to 2/0 hook

24 kg trace

Minnow Lure

Deep Diving Minnow

Live bait

Fly fishing is successful

BONITO

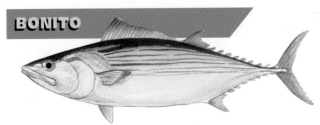

Scientific name: *Sarda orientalis*. Also known as 'Oriental' Bonito.

Description: Similar to Australian bonito but differs in separate range and Oriental bonito has no prominent stripes on the lower part of its body. Grows to 3.5 kilograms.

Fishing: Similar methods for Australian bonito. Can be very common in inshore waters, giving a pleasant surprise to shore based casters fishing for tailor and herring. The Oriental bonito should be bled after capture and is only moderately regarded as a food fish.

BARRACUDA

Scientific name: *Sphyraena barracuda*. Also known as Great barracuda, giant barracuda, giant sea pike.

Description: The most remarkable feature of the barracuda is its fearsome teeth. There are two pairs of enlarged canines on the upper jaw and one pair of enlarged canines on the lower jaw. There are other large, backward pointing teeth in both jaws.

The body is long and cylindrical with approximately 18 grayish cross bands on the back above the lateral line. These bands on the back and the more heavy body differentiate the barracuda from the similar snook, which is generally found outside of the range of the barracuda. The barracuda reaches 1.8 m and nearly 25 kilograms.

BREAM, BLACK

Scientific name: *Acanthopagrus butcheri*. Also known as Bream, blue nosed bream.

Description: The black bream is a very highly sought after angling species of the estuaries of southern WA. The mouth is fairly small with rows of peg like teeth and crushing plates on the palate. It reaches a maximum size of around 3.5 kg, but a specimen over 1 kg is highly regarded.

Fishing: This is one of the most sought after species in Australia. They are most commonly fished with a light line of 3 – 5 kilograms. Bait running reels on shorter rods are frequently used. Bream generally bite best on a rising tide and after dark but many quality fish, including on lures, are taken during the day and in ambush sites on the bottom half of the tide. Bream can be timid biters so as little weight as possible should be used and any sinker must run freely. Best baits are river prawn, although beach and blood worms, pipi, anchovy or blue sardine and flesh baits also work extremely well. When bream bite, it is important to let them run up to a metre before setting the hook. The bream will then run strongly for the nearest cover and many fish are lost on this initial surge. They are also excellent lure or soft plastic targets.

Rigs and Tactics:

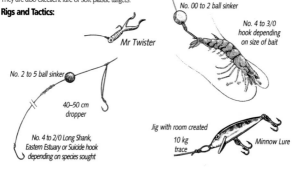

Mr Twister

No. 00 to 2 ball sinker

No. 4 to 3/0 hook depending on size of bait

No. 2 to 5 ball sinker

40–50 cm dropper

No. 4 to 2/0 Long Shank, Eastern Estuary or Suicide hook depending on species sought

Jig with room created

10 kg trace

Minnow Lure

saltwater species

CHINAMAN FISH

Caution:

POISONOUS

Scientific name: *Symphorus nematophorus*. Also known as Threadfin sea perch (juveniles), galloper. Should not be confused with the Chinaman cod (*Epinephelus rivulatus*) which is a common and safe catch in northern Western Australia.

Description: Juveniles look substantially different from adults with blue stripes on a yellow background and extended soft dorsal ray filaments. Fins are reddish pink.

Adults lack extended filaments and are reddish with dark vertical bars. Adults have a stout body and a row of scales on the cheeks. The Chinaman fish also possesses a deep pit on the upper snout, immediately before the eyes.

An extremely hard fighting fish that is considered safe to eat in moderate quantities in WA.

COBBLER (CATFISH, ESTUARY)

Scientific name: *Cnidoglanis macrocephalus*. Also known as Cobbler.

Description: A very long eel-tailed species found in muddy or weedy estuaries. They are most commonly caught near washed up weeds or near weed patches. When spawning, cobbler form balls of fish which can be spotted by the muddy water which surrounds them. They make nests in weed.

The pectoral and dorsal fins possess a large spine which contains a poison gland. A puncture wound causes a great deal of pain. Treatment is with hot water or compresses to cook the protein.

Fishing: Cobbler are actively fished for in many areas with light bottom rigs and baits of prawn or worms. They are good fighters but must be handled carefully when being unhooked. In some areas, estuary catfish are taken by gidgee or spear in the shallows at night. In spite of their appearance, estuary catfish are excellent eating and are highly prized in Western Australia.

Rigs and Tactics:

No. 00 to 2 ball sinker

No. 4 to 3/0 hook depending on size of bait

No. 1 to 4 bean sinker

Brass ring or small swivel

30–50 cm

No. 1/0 to 6/0 hook

No. 00 to 2 ball sinker

No. 4 to 1 Suicide or baitholder hook

No. 6 to 4 Baitholder hook

COBIA

Scientific name: *Rachycentron canadus*. Also known as Cobe, black kingfish, black king, crab-eater, sergeant fish, lemon fish.

Description: A large pelagic species reaching over 2 m and 60 kilograms. Frequently mistaken initially for a shark in the water due to its high dorsal fin and large, dark pectoral fins. Often found with manta rays.

They have a relatively pointy head with the mouth at the middle of the front of the head. They have a white or creamy belly and a white stripe on their sides which may fade after death. They also have very short dorsal spines before the high soft dorsal fin. Other fins, except pelvic are dark and the overall colour is chocolate brown to black.

COD, BREAKSEA

Scientific name: *Epinephelides armatus*. Also known as Black-arse cod, black arse, tiger cod.

Description: Relatively common inshore species often found around bommies and shallow reefs. Colour varies but can be brown to yellow with dusky black fins. The eye is a bright red and the anus is found in a large black spot, leading to the common names.

Fishing: This species is commonly taken in mixed reef catches. Breaksea cod have a large mouth and will take large baits intended for other species. Standard reef paternoster rigs and baits work well with cut baits, prawn, pilchard and squid working well.

This species is good eating.

Rigs and Tactics:

Solid brass ring
Solid brass ring
30–40 cm
No. 2/0 to 8/0 hook
Main line
60–120 g star sinker

Solid brass ring
Solid brass ring
30–50 kg trace
1 metre
100-500 g barrel sinker

Dropper loop 30 cm
Main line
No. 3/0 hook - Limerick, Suicide or Viking pattern
50 cm
30–50 cm
Dropper loop 15 cm
1/2 kg snapper sinker
No. 3/0 hook

COD, CHINAMAN

Scientific name: *Epinephelus rivulatus*. Also known as Chinaman rockcod, Charlie Court cod.

Description: A fairly small but attractive cod species with the fairly typical large mouth and long dorsal fin with lobed soft dorsal. The Chinaman cod can be distinguished by 4 or 5 prominent broad bars down the sides, although these can be very pale in specimens taken near sandy or broken bottoms. There are frequently white blotches on the head. The Chinaman cod is similar to the black-tipped rockcod, but lacks the distinctive black to reddish tips to the dorsal spines. The Chinaman cod reaches 45 cm and around 1.3 kg but is frequently caught at around 30 centimetres.

Fishing: The Chinaman cod is a common table catch in the north-west of the state. It is taken on standard reef rigs and baits of cut fish, pilchard, squid and octopus. In places like Ningaloo Reef, the Chinaman cod is a common capture which makes pleasant eating and compensates for the times when north-west snapper and other more prized fish are less accommodating. Chinaman cod are most frequently taken from deeper reefs where the heavier lines and larger hooks tend to sandbag a reasonable fight.

Rigs and Tactics:

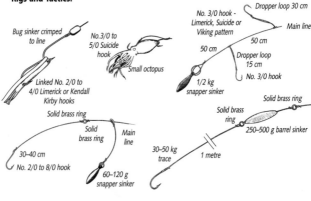

COD, VERMICULAR

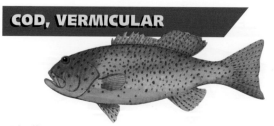

Scientific name: *Plectropomus oligocanthus.* Also known as lined coral trout, vermicular trout

Description: The various coral trout species being coral trout, bar-cheek coral trout and vermicular cod are all easily confused. The vermicular cod tends to be more bright red or orange red, while coral trout can be a dark brick red. The vermicular cod has larger blue dots on its body and some are likely to be elongated dorsally. The spots on the head are fewer and larger than with the coral trout and are not elongated laterally as with the bar-cheek coral trout. The vermicular cod also has a higher soft part of the dorsal fin, but this characteristic is most useful when comparing another trout. The vermicular cod is found on off-shore reefs more commonly and reaches 56 cm in length whereas the coral trout reaches 75 cm and the bar-cheek coral trout 70 centimetres.

Fishing: Like all the coral trouts, the vermicular cod is first rate eating. It is taken on standard reef fishing rigs. Its preference for coral reefs and a strong first run makes heavier line more necessary. The vermicular cod will also rise to take trolled lures and bait tipped jigs also work extremely well. Best baits include cut fish baits, pilchard, garfish, squid, octopus and large prawns.

Rigs and Tactics:

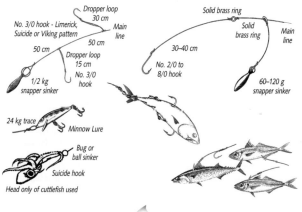

No. 3/0 hook - Limerick, Suicide or Viking pattern

Dropper loop 30 cm

Main line

50 cm

50 cm

Dropper loop 15 cm

No. 3/0 hook

1/2 kg snapper sinker

Solid brass ring

Solid brass ring

Main line

30–40 cm

No. 2/0 to 8/0 hook

60–120 g snapper sinker

24 kg trace

Minnow Lure

Bug or ball sinker

Suicide hook

Head only of cuttlefish used

COD, ESTUARY

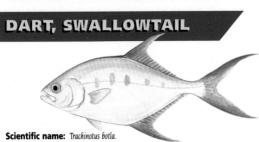

Scientific name: *Epinephelus coioides*. (Frequently misidentified as *Epinephelus malabaricus* or *Epinephelus tauvina*) Also known as Greasy cod, spotted cod, north-west groper, estuary rock cod, gold spotted rock cod, spotted river cod, orange-spotted cod.

Description: The estuary cod is one of the largest and most common cod found in tropical estuaries and coastal reefs reaching a length of over 2 m and 230 kilograms. The estuary cod is olive-green to brown with scattered brown spots. The back has four to six darker blotches which fade with age to uniform brown colour. Similar to Queensland groper but the estuary cod has three opercular spines equal distances apart. The tail is rounded.

DART, SWALLOWTAIL

Scientific name: *Trachinotus botla*.

Also known as Dart, Common Dart, Swallowtail, Southern swallowtail.

Description: From the same family as trevally, the swallowtail dart bears some external similarities and shares the same tenacious side-on fight. Dart are handsome fish with a deeply forked tail. The dorsal fin is set well back on the fish and the first few dorsal and anal rays are elongated. The swallowtail dart has between one and five large spots on the side of the fish. The swallowtail dart is distinguished from the black spotted dart whose spots are smaller than the pupil of the eye. The snub nosed dart has no spots on its sides and a much more blunt, rounded head profile.

The swallowtail dart grows to 60 cm but is often caught at smaller sizes. A dart of larger than 1 kg is noteworthy, and their strong fight makes up for their lack of size.

DHUFISH

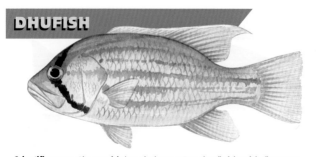

Scientific name: *Glaucosoma hebraicum*. Also known as Westralian dhufish, jewfish, dhuie, jewie.

Description: The dhufish is an attractive relative of the pearl perch, and is the most prized species for Western Australian boat anglers. The dhufish has a distinctive eye stripe. A dorsal ray, especially in males can be elongated. Juvenile dhufish have distinctive horizontal black stripes. It is found in depths of up to 140 m or so. Recent research indicates high mortality of fish taken in greater than 50 m or so but using depth release sinkers to rapidly return the fish to depth is strongly recommended. Dhufish have a very large mouth and can take a big bait. Dhufish can reach 27 kg and every year a number of fish of 22 kg are taken.

Fishing: Tagging studies show very limited movement of dhufish. Dhufish take baits fished on standard deep water two hook rigs. They take whole fish, squid, pilchard or live fish if available. Whiting heads are a favourite bait. Anglers drift lumps in waters from 10 – 70 m in depth for mixed bags with dhufish the most prized species. Taken from deep water, a big dhufish feels like the bottom, but the fight diminishes as the fish nears the surface. This fish is arguably the best eating species in Western Australia.

Rigs and Tactics:

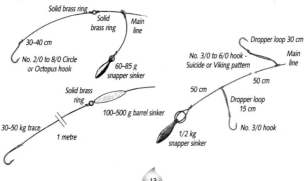

Solid brass ring
Solid brass ring
Main line
30–40 cm
No. 2/0 to 8/0 Circle or Octopus hook
60–85 g snapper sinker

Dropper loop 30 cm
Main line
No. 3/0 to 6/0 hook - Suicide or Viking pattern
50 cm
50 cm
Dropper loop 15 cm
No. 3/0 hook

Solid brass ring
100–500 g barrel sinker
30–50 kg trace
1 metre
1/2 kg snapper sinker

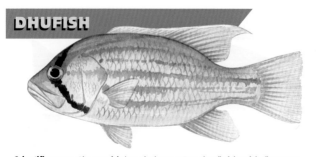
saltwater species

DRUMMER, SILVER

Scientific name: *Kyphosus cornelii*. Also known as western buffalo bream, buffie.

Description: The silver drummer is a large schooling fish growing to 12 kg which offers better sport than eating. These mainly herbivorous fish are found in surge zones and near inshore reefs. They are dusky silver with fairly prominent lengthwise bands. The lips appear more prominent than in rock blackfish and the head is more pointed.

Fishing: Silver drummer are fished for with sea cabbage, bread, and prawns. They can take bluebait or pilchards intended for other species. Silver drummer are caught under floats in the surge zones or on lightly weighted baits fished near inshore reefs. Berley of bread, or weed works well.

Silver drummer fight hard but fair and make poor eating even if bled and cleaned immediately. Be careful when handling the silver drummer as it often defecates when anglers try to unhook it.

Rigs and Tactics:

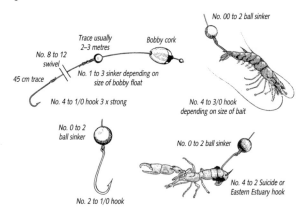

No. 00 to 2 ball sinker

Trace usually 2–3 metres

Bobby cork

No. 8 to 12 swivel

No. 1 to 3 sinker depending on size of bobby float

45 cm trace

No. 4 to 1/0 hook 3 x strong

No. 4 to 3/0 hook depending on size of bait

No. 0 to 2 ball sinker

No. 0 to 2 ball sinker

No. 2 to 1/0 hook

No. 4 to 2 Suicide or Eastern Estuary hook

EMPEROR, RED

Scientific name: *Lutjanus sebae*. Also known as Government bream, red kelp.

Description: A striking and highly prized reef fish. The red emperor is a schooling fish which means that fishing can be fast and furious, but this valuable species can be taken in large numbers in commercial fish traps and trawls.

The red emperor changes appearance as it grows. Juveniles are known as Government bream as the three striking bands resemble a convict's broad arrow. This pattern fades with age and fish over 13 kg become a uniform scarlet or salmon pink. The reddish fins are narrowly edged with white. The cheeks are scaled and there is a deep notch in the lower edge of the pre-operculum (inner cheekbone).

Fishing: Red emperor fight extremely well, even when taken from deeper waters where they are increasingly taken. The red emperor can reach 22 kg and more than a metre in length which increases their allure.

Red emperor prefer moving water in channels near deeper reefs. As a result, they can be taken on drifts between reef patches in seemingly open ground. They tend to form schools of similar sized fish and are partial to cut fish baits, octopus, squid or pilchards. The red emperor is excellent eating even in the larger sizes and is considered safe from ciguatera.

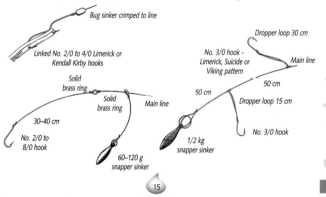

Bug sinker crimped to line

Linked No. 2/0 to 4/0 Limerick or Kendall Kirby hooks

Solid brass ring

Solid brass ring

Main line

30–40 cm

No. 2/0 to 8/0 hook

60–120 g snapper sinker

Dropper loop 30 cm

No. 3/0 hook - Limerick, Suicide or Viking pattern

Main line

50 cm

50 cm

Dropper loop 15 cm

1/2 kg snapper sinker

No. 3/0 hook

EMPEROR, LONG NOSED

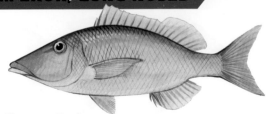

Scientific name: *Lethrinus olivaceous.*

Description: One of the largest species of emperor, reaching 10 kg and a metre in length. Easily distinguished by the long sloping head and the generally greenish colouration. There is generally a red line on the lips of these fish and the dorsal fin may have red spots.

Fishing: Standard reef fishing tackle and rigs will account for this hard fighting species. Can be found on inshore or offshore reefs and its larger size can cause extra troubles for angling. Fresh baits and strong leaders are recommended. Fish flesh, squid, octopus, pilchard or live baits account for the majority of these fish. Highly regarded as a food fish.

EMPEROR, SPANGLED

Scientific name: *Lethrinus nebulosus.* Also known as Nor-west snapper, Nor'wester, yellow sweetlip, sand snapper, sand bream.

Description: A striking member of the sweetlip group. This species is easily identified by the blue spots on each scale and the blue bars on the cheek. This species can reach 86 cm and 6.5 kg and is considered very good eating.

Fishing: The spangled emperor is generally taken adjacent to coral or rock reefs over gravel or sand bottoms. They frequent lagoons and coral cays and can be taken from the beach in Western Australia where there are reef patches nearby. They are particularly active at night.

The spangled emperor can be taken with standard reef rigs, but as they are most common in water under 15 metres deep, lighter rigs and berley can be successful. Use cut fish, pilchards, squid, octopus, crab or prawn baits. Spangled emperor will take jigs or minnow lures either trolled or cast in areas near reefs where spangled emperor feed.

EMPEROR, SWEETLIP

Scientific name: *Lethrinus miniatus. (formerly Lethrinus chrysostomus)* Also known as Sweetlip, lipper, red-throat.

Description: The sweetlip emperor is a common emperor species. It is identified by orange areas around the eyes, a bright red dorsal fin, and a red patch at the base of the pectoral fins. The inside of the mouth is red. Some fish have a series of brown vertical bands but many fish are a uniform colour. This species reaches a metre and 9 kg but is more common from 1 to 2.5 kilograms.

Fishing: Found in reef country, but frequently taken from areas between reefs, the sweetlip emperor can be berleyed up and large catches taken from the feeding school. The sweetlip emperor fights well and is able to dive to the bottom and break off an unwary angler.

These fish respond well to oily fleshed baits such as pilchard or mackerel, but when feeding can be caught on most baits including cut baits, squid, octopus, prawn and crab. Sweetlip emperor are highly regarded food fish.

FLATHEAD, SOUTHERN BLUE-SPOTTED

Scientific name: *Platycephalus speculator.* Also known as Southern flathead, yank flathead, Castelnau's flathead, southern dusky flathead, bluespot flathead, long nose flathead, shovelnose flathead.

Description: This flathead can be distinguished on the basis of grey-green spots on the top half of the tail and 3 to 5 large black spots on the lower portion, surrounded by white or off-white. This species also has only one dorsal spine compared with two for many other flathead. The southern blue-spotted flathead can reach a maximum size of nearly 8 kg, although any fish of 3 kg is rare and it is much more common at around a kilogram.

Fishing: The southern blue-spot flathead ambushes prey wherever possible. This species can occasionally be found over weed patches or around the edges of weeds. It is not as commonly taken on lures and can be a welcome bonus when fishing for King George whiting or when baits sink through berley fishing for herring and garfish. The southern blue-spotted flathead is good eating.

FLATHEAD, BAR-TAIL

Scientific name: *Platycephalus endrachtensis*. Also known as Western estuary flathead.

Description: Readily identified by the tail fin which has black and white horizontal stripes on the tail with a yellow blotch at the top of the fin. The similar northern sand flathead grows to 45 cm but has no yellow tail blotch. Found on sand, gravel, light rock and silt bottoms.

The bar-tailed flathead can reaching 1 m in length, but in the Swan estuary (not found further south) where it is particularly targeted, any fish above 55 cm is noteworthy and most fish are between 30 and 45 centimetres. Takes lures and jigs particularly well.

Fishing: The bar-tail flathead can be fished with similar methods as for dusky flathead. They will readily take lures such as minnows, jigs and wobblers and they will also take flies well. Bar-tail flathead bite on blue sardines, whitebait, prawns, pipi, squid and crab or pilchard pieces. These should be fished with a light weight on a fairly long trace. A mobile approach works best, fishing the edges of drop-offs especially on a falling tide or on the deeper side during low tide and the early rising tide. Trolling these same areas will also take fish.

Bar-tail flathead make very good eating and is a reward for one of casting near sandy drop offs which is the most enjoyable and relaxing forms of fishing.

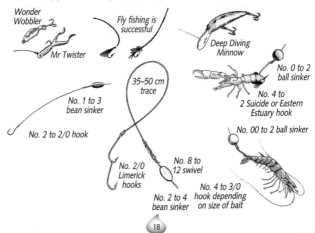

Wonder Wobbler

Mr Twister

Fly fishing is successful

Deep Diving Minnow

No. 0 to 2 ball sinker

No. 1 to 3 bean sinker

35–50 cm trace

No. 4 to 2 Suicide or Eastern Estuary hook

No. 2 to 2/0 hook

No. 00 to 2 ball sinker

No. 2/0 Limerick hooks

No. 8 to 12 swivel

No. 2 to 4 bean sinker

No. 4 to 3/0 hook depending on size of bait

saltwater Species

GROPER, BALDCHIN

Scientific name: *Choerodon rubescens*.
Also known as Tusk-fish, baldie, bluebone.

Description: The baldchin groper is one of the largest tusk-fish species reaching 90 cm and 14 kilograms. All tusk-fish have prominent protruding, tusk-like teeth in both jaws. This species is easily identified by the white chin which is more prominent in males which are larger. The pectoral fin is yellow with a pale bluish base. The tusk-fish bones have a pale bluish colour, leading to one of their common names. This species is found on inshore reefs to a depth of 40 m, with smaller fish generally found in shallower waters.

Fishing: An excellent fighting fish and one of Western Australia's premier eating fish, the baldchin groper is highly sought after. Baldchin groper are taken with standard reef fishing rigs and baits, although crabs can be particularly productive if available. Baldchin will also take prawns, octopus, squid, crabs and, less frequently, fish baits but there can be times when baldchin can be finicky feeders, so it pays to experiment with baits and rigs. Spearfishers can have a significant impact especially on small populations on isolated reefs.

Rigs and Tactics:

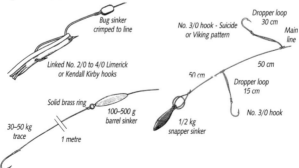

GROPER, WESTERN BLUE

Scientific name: *Achoerodus gouldii*. Also known as giant pigfish, blue tank.

Description: The western blue groper can reach 40 kg. The blue gropers are easily identified by their size, often brilliant colours, their fleshy lips, heavy scales and peg like teeth.

Blue groper prefer turbulent rocky shorelines or inshore bomboras. This species is protected from spearfishing.

Fishing: Blue groper present a real test for shore based anglers. They can be taken on prawns and squid, fresh crabs, and especially the rock crabs found in the intertidal areas. Crabs are easily the best bait. Heavy rods and line and extra strong hooks are required for these hard, dirty fighters. A groper should not be given its head as it will bury you in the nearest cave or under any rock ledge. Small to medium blue groper are good eating, but large ones are dry and the flesh coarse. Some huge fish are taken on deeper reefs on the south coast of WA.

Rigs and Tactics:

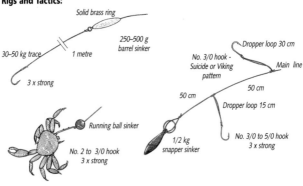

Solid brass ring

30–50 kg trace   1 metre

250–500 g barrel sinker

3 x strong

Dropper loop 30 cm

No. 3/0 hook - Suicide or Viking pattern

Main line

50 cm

50 cm

Dropper loop 15 cm

Running ball sinker

No. 2 to 3/0 hook 3 x strong

1/2 kg snapper sinker

No. 3/0 to 5/0 hook 3 x strong

HARLEQUIN FISH

Scientific name: *Othos dentex*. Also known as harlequin cod, Chinese lantern, tiger cod

Description: A truly stunning species which superficially resembles the coral trout of much more tropical waters but is a bit more long and slender. The harlequin fish can have blue spots on the head of variable shape which may extend to the chin. The overall colour can vary in a similar fashion to coral trout but is more commonly red or orange and much less frequently brick red. The harlequin fish has yellow or creamy yellow blotches on the lower sides of the fish. The tail is slightly convex whereas with the coral trout species the tail is either square or concave. These species do not overlap in range but can be confused if seen together in a fish shop.

The harlequin fish inhabits coastal reefs in inshore waters. It is inquisitive and can be susceptible to spearfishing pressure. The harlequin fish can grow to 75 centimetres.

Standard reef fishing techniques rigs and baits will take harlequin fish. As they can be found in shallow reef areas, lighter sinkers and rigs work as well. The harlequin can be taken on squid, octopus, and pilchard or cut flesh baits. This species is considered very good eating.

Rigs and Tactics:

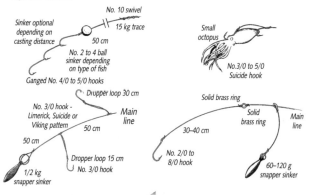

HERRING, AUSTRALIAN

Scientific name: *Arripis georgiana*. Also known as Tommy rough, tommy, ruff, bull herring, Western herring.

Description: A pretty and highly sought after species, the Australian herring is not a 'true' herring from the family Clupidae. Although the Australian herring can reach 40 cm, they are commonly caught at between 22 and 28 centimetres. The herring is similar to a juvenile Australian salmon, but the herring has a larger eye, black tips on the ends of the tail fin lobes and no black blotch at the base of the pectoral fin. The herring's scales feel rough when rubbed towards the head whereas an Australian salmon feels smooth which gives rise to the common name 'ruff'.

Fishing: Australian herring specialists can turn angling for these scrappy little fighters to an art form. Standard rigs include a wooden blob (float) whose hole is filled with pollard and pilchard oil, a reasonably long trace and a bait of maggot, prawn, squid or blue bait. When biting freely, Australian herring are taken on pieces of green drinking straw.

Herring are an inshore schooling fish which is commonly taken from rock groynes and beaches and are attracted to berley slicks when boat angling, especially inshore around shallow sea grass beds. Best berley includes bread, pollard, finely chopped fish scraps and chip pieces leftover from the local fish and chip shop. Herring are also taken on lures, with Halco wobblers and Tassie Devils or any small lure with red working well. On lures, herring jump as well as their cousins the salmon and although some throw the hooks, they are terrific fun. Herring are also very good eating.

Rigs and Tactics:

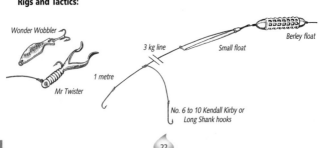

Wonder Wobbler

Mr Twister

3 kg line

1 metre

Small float

Berley float

No. 6 to 10 Kendall Kirby or Long Shank hooks

JEWFISH, BLACK

Scientific name: *Protonibea diacanthus*. Also known as Black jew, Spotted croaker, Spotted jew, Blotched jewfish, black mulloway, northern mulloway.

Description: The black mulloway is a large and prized northern mulloway species, growing to 40 kg and more than 1.5 metres. The range is important as there are few locations where black jewfish and mulloway can be taken together. The black jewfish has two prominent anal spines whereas the mulloway has a small second anal spine. The soft dorsal fin has 22 to 25 rays as opposed to 28 to 31 rays for the smaller and lighter coloured silver jewfish (*Nibea soldado*) of north-eastern waters which also has white ventral fins.

The black jewfish has a grey to blackish colour. Young fish have black spots on the back, dorsal and tail fins which fade in adult fish. Excellent eating.

Rigs and Tactics:

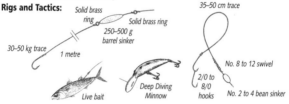

LONGTOM, SLENDER

Scientific name: *Stronylura leiura*. Also known as common longtom.

Description: The common name is quite apt as this is a slender and sleek species. The slender longtom is most easily separated from other longtoms by the bar along the base of the gill cover which can fade after death. The jaws are elongated and filled with needle sharp teeth which makes hooking difficult.

The slender longtom is most commonly found in coastal waters and can be found in large bays and estuaries. This species can reach 110 cm but is most frequently encountered in estuaries at a smaller size.

Saltwater Species

KINGFISH, YELLLOWTAIL

Scientific name: *Seriola lalandi*. Also known as Kingie, yellowtail, hoodlum and bandit.

Description: The yellowtail kingfish is a beautiful, powerful fish which has a large, deeply forked tail. The back and upper sides are dark, purply blue while the lower part of the body is white. These two distinctive colours are separated by a yellow band which varies in width and intensity from fish to fish. The tail is a bright yellow. This can be a large fish reaching 2 m and more than 50 kg. Any yellowtail kingfish over 20 kg will be a memorable capture.

Fishing: The yellowtail kingfish is a brutal, dirty fighter which will fully test the skill of the angler and the quality of their gear. The first run of a kingfish is straight towards the nearest bottom obstruction to cut off an unwary angler. Kingfish will take a wide variety of lures such as minnow lures, soft plastics and flies. Vertical jigging with metal lures can be deadly. They will take a range of whole and cut fish baits, squid, octopus and cuttlefish but there are occasions when they can be finicky. At other times yellowtail kingfish will strike at bare hooks. Live bait is almost certain to attract any kingfish in the area.

Kingfish were previously considered average eating, but they have been increasingly recognised as a quality fish, including as sashimi. Large fish are worse eating and can have worms in the flesh.

Rigs and Tactics:

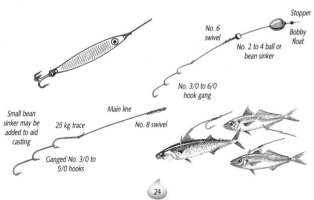

MACKEREL, BROAD-BARRED SPANISH

Scientific name: *Scomberomorus semifasciatus*. Also known as Grey mackerel, tiger mackerel, broad barred mackerel.

Range: Shark Bay northwards and around tropical waters to northern NSW.

Description: A similar species to the more common and generally larger Spanish mackerel, they can be readily identified by the much larger soft dorsal and anal fins. The bars are much broader and fewer in number with live fish, but they fade significantly on death, giving rise to the marketing name of grey mackerel. The broad-barred Spanish mackerel reaches 1.2 m and 8 kg but is commonly caught at 1 – 3 kg from inshore waters.

Fishing: Like its larger cousin, the broad-barred Spanish mackerel readily takes small minnow or chrome lures and whole or cut fish baits. Live baits work extremely well. This species fights well, particularly on light line but is not as highly regarded a food fish as the Spanish mackerel.

Rigs and Tactics:

24 kg trace — Minnow Lure

Wire Trace

Metal Lure

Small bean sinker may be added to aid casting

25 kg trace
Ganged No. 3/0 to 5/0
Limerick hooks

Main line — No. 8 swivel

No. 3/0 to 5/0 hook gang

No. 10 swivel

No. 2 to 4 ball or bean sinker

Stopper — Bobby float

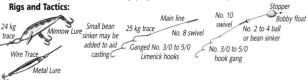

MACKEREL, FRIGATE

Scientific name: *Auxis thazard*. Also known as Little tuna.

Description: A handsome fish which can reach 60 cm and around 5 kilograms. The frigate mackerel possesses the distinctive broken oblique lines above the lateral line and no markings below the lateral line. It can be easily separated from the similar mackerel tuna as the frigate mackerel has a wide gap between the two dorsal fins, no black spots near the ventral fins and a more slender body. The frigate mackerel can form large shoals in coastal or inshore waters.

saltwater species

MACKEREL, SHARK

Scientific name: *Grammatorcynus bicarinatus*.

Also known as Scaly mackerel, large-scaled tunny, salmon mackerel.

Description: A sought after fish found on shallow reef areas throughout its range. This species has a distinguishing double lateral line which divides at the pectoral fin and joins again at the tail base. The belly displays dark spots and the eye is relatively small, especially compared to the similar double lined (or scad) mackerel. The scales of the shark mackerel come away in large sheets.

The name shark mackerel comes from a distinctive ammonia smell (shark-like) when the fish is cleaned but which disappears with cooking. The shark mackerel can reach 1.3 m and 11 kilograms.

Fishing: Shark mackerel are good lure prospects, rising to take minnow or spoon type lure where they put up a determined surface based fight. Shark mackerel are also taken on drifted whole or cut fish baits and live baits, although shark mackerel are not the general target species with live baits in tropical waters. The shark mackerel makes reasonable eating but the quality is improved by skinning the fillets.

Rigs and Tactics:

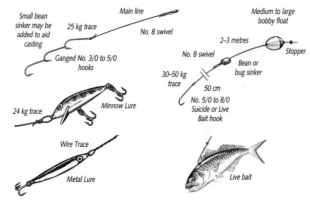

Small bean sinker may be added to aid casting

Main line

25 kg trace

No. 8 swivel

Ganged No. 3/0 to 5/0 hooks

Medium to large bobby float

2–3 metres

No. 8 swivel

Stopper

Bean or bug sinker

30–50 kg trace

50 cm

No. 5/0 to 8/0 Suicide or Live Bait hook

24 kg trace

Minnow Lure

Wire Trace

Metal Lure

Live bait

MACKEREL, SPANISH

Scientific name: *Scomberomorus commerson*. Also known as Narrow-barred Spanish mackerel, blue mackerel, tanguigue, Spaniard, seer, seerfish.

Description: The Spanish mackerel is a highly sought after and valued species capable of reaching 2.35 m and 42 kilograms. It is commonly taken from 5 – 15 kilograms. Smaller fish travel in pods of similar sized fish. The Spanish mackerel is similar to the wahoo but has fewer dorsal spines (15 – 18 versus 23 – 27) in a shorter dorsal fin. The upper jaw of the Spanish mackerel has an obvious external bone which extends to at least the middle of the eye, while in the wahoo there is no obvious bone and the upper jaw extends to the front edge of the eye. The Spanish mackerel is found in coastal waters, frequently in the vicinity of reefs.

Fishing: Spanish mackerel will aggressively take trolled lures and baits. Minnow lures, spoons and feathered lures run at 5 – 7 knots work best, while trolled garfish, slimy mackerel or other fish at 3 – 5 knots will take good catches. Spanish mackerel will also take drifted live, whole or cut baits. Land based fishermen drift large baits under balloons to take large fish. A wire trace is an effective counter to the sharp teeth.

The Spanish mackerel is an excellent sport fish, particularly on light line, as it runs strongly and occasionally jumps in its attempts to escape. Spanish mackerel can actively feed at different depths, so lures and baits which target a wide range will more quickly locate fish.

It is a highly regarded food fish, but does not freeze particularly well. The quality is much better when the fish is filleted.

Rigs and tactics:

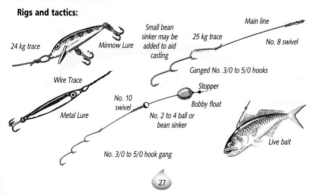

24 kg trace — Minnow Lure

Small bean sinker may be added to aid casting

Main line

25 kg trace — No. 8 swivel

Ganged No. 3/0 to 5/0 hooks

Wire Trace

Metal Lure

No. 10 swivel

Stopper

Bobby float

No. 2 to 4 ball or bean sinker

Live bait

No. 3/0 to 5/0 hook gang

MACKEREL, QUEENSLAND SCHOOL

Scientific name: *Scomberomorus queenslandicus*. Also known as School mackerel, doggie mackerel, blotched mackerel, shiny mackerel.

Description: The Queensland school mackerel is a schooling species which frequents inshore areas. The Queensland school mackerel can reach a metre in length and a weight of 12 kilograms. However they are commonly encountered from 1.5 to 4 kg. This species is easily identified by the large dark spots on the sides and the black then white areas on the first dorsal fin. The pectoral fin is also smaller and more pointed than in the broad-barred Spanish mackerel.

Fishing: Schools of Queensland school mackerel can be berleyed close to the boat and taken with live or whole dead or fresh cut bait. These fish will take lures but can be finicky. Queensland school mackerel can patrol close to the shore and can be a surprise catch from tropical beaches and creek mouths, but they can bite off lures or baits intended for other species. The Queensland school mackerel is a top table fish if filleted.

Rigs and Tactics:

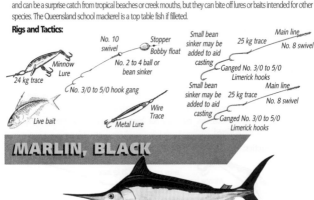

MARLIN, BLACK

Scientific name: *Makaira indica*.
Also known as Giant black marlin, silver marlin.

Description: A magnificent blue water billfish capable of reaching a length of nearly 5 m and 850 kilograms. The black marlin is readily distinguished by its rigid pectoral fins which cannot be laid next to body in any black marlin and are completely rigid in all fish over 50 kg. In this fairly heavy bodied fish, the start of the second dorsal is forward to the start of the second anal fin. Black marlin are most commonly found in blue water, with fish moving southwards as far as Augusta with the warmer currents. Black marlin are found above deep structure along current lines and where baitfish aggregations are prevalent.

MAHI MAHI

Scientific name: *Coryphaena hippurus*. Also known as Dolphin, dolphin fish, common dolphinfish, dorado.

Description: The mahi mahi is one of the most beautiful fish in the ocean when lit up, with bright yellow to blue colouration and brilliant blue flecks over most of the body and fins. The fantastic colours fade to a washed out grey after death. Mature male or 'bull' mahi mahi have a prominent high forehead and tend to be more brightly coloured. Females have a more streamlined head profile.

The species is easily recognised in photographs due to its shape and brilliant colours. Other diagnostic features include the very long dorsal and anal fins and the deeply veed tail.

Mahi mahi are arguably the fastest growing species in the ocean, growing as much as a centimetre a day when food is plentiful. Mahi mahi can reach 2 m and more than 20 kg but are frequently taken in Australia from 2 to 10 kilograms. In Western Australia, mahi mahi are first found in oceanic waters at less than a kilogram and within five months, those that have not been caught are more than 10 kilograms.

Rigs and Tactics:

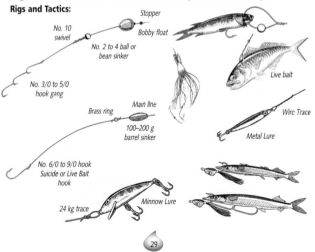

MANGROVE JACK

Scientific name: *Lutjanus argentimaculatus*. Also known as Jacks, red bream, dog bream, red perch, reef red bream, purple sea perch, creek red bream.

Description: The mangrove jack is best known for its destruction of fishing tackle in tidal creeks, but these tend to be juvenile or small adult fish. The largest specimens are taken on offshore reefs to a depth of 100 metres. Mangrove jack can reach more than 1.2 m and a weight of 15 kg and live more than 50 years. Fish in inshore waters are a real handful at 1 – 3 kilograms.

The mangrove jack is often confused with the red bass, which is a much more notorious ciguatera species, especially if caught on reefs . The mangrove jack has a taller dorsal fin, a lack of lengthwise stripes on its side and absence of black on the fins. Mangrove jacks lack the distinctive pit before the eye of the red bass.

Fishing: Mangrove jack are arguably the toughest and dirtiest fighters (pound for pound) in Australian waters. They will dash out and engulf a lure or bait and break off an unwary angler on the nearest snag before they realise the strike has been made. As a result, mangrove jacks require quality, well maintained gear and tight drags. They can destroy cheap equipment as they dive into snags.

Mangrove jacks like tough dirty cover although they can be found in deeper holes in tidal waters where they are a bit easier to handle. Diving lures, spinner baits, jigs and flies work well for jacks. They will take cut or whole fish baits, prawns, crabs and especially live baits. The strike is savage and a prelude to the action to come. Mangrove jacks taken on offshore reefs put up a strong light, but the heavier gear usually used for tropical reef fishing gives a better chance of landing these fish.

Mangrove jacks should be handled carefully as their dorsal and opercular spines can create a nasty wound. They are a hardy fish which survives handling well. The mangrove jack is good eating.

Rigs and Tactics:

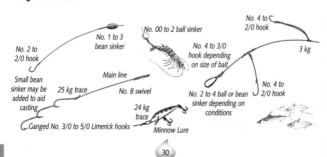

No. 2 to 2/0 hook

No. 1 to 3 bean sinker

No. 00 to 2 ball sinker

No. 4 to 2/0 hook

3 kg

Small bean sinker may be added to aid casting

Main line

25 kg trace

No. 8 swivel

No. 4 to 3/0 hook depending on size of bait

No. 2 to 4 ball or bean sinker depending on conditions

No. 4 to 2/0 hook

Ganged No. 3/0 to 5/0 Limerick hooks

24 kg trace

Minnow Lure

MULLOWAY

Scientific name: *Argyrosomus japonicus*. Also known as butterfish, river kingfish, silver kingfish.

Small fish to around 3 kg are generally referred to as soapies due to their rather bland or soapy taste. Fish from 3 – 8 kg are frequently known as Schoolies as they are often encountered in schools which decrease in number as the size increases.

Description: Mulloway are a large and highly prized species found in estuaries, embayments and inshore ocean waters throughout its range. The mulloway can vary in colour from dark bronze to silver and there may be red or purple tinges, but a silver ocean mulloway is a stunning fish.

The mulloway has large scales and a generous mouth. A line of silvery spots follows the lateral line in live fish which glows under artificial lights as do the eyes which shine a bright red. A conspicuous black spot is just above the pectoral fin. The tail fin is convex (rounded outwards).

Mulloway can reach 1.8 m and more than 60 kg, but any fish over 25 kg is worth long term boasting rights for the angler.

Rigs and Tactics:

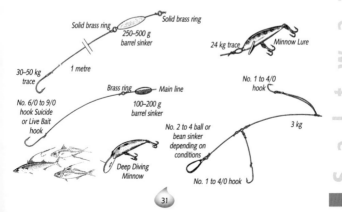

MULLET, YELLOW-EYE

Scientific name: *Aldrichetta forsteri*. Also known as Pilch or pilchard, estuary mullet, freshwater mullet, yelloweye.

Description: A very common species of southern estuaries and embayments. Yellow-eye mullet also move on or just off beaches near estuaries during winter in Western Australia. The bright yellow eye, without the gelatinous eye covering, is diagnostic. This species also has small teeth in both jaws and 12 rays in the anal fin. The yellow-eye mullet grows to 50 cm and more than 1 kg, but is most common at around 30 centimetres.

Fishing: In Western Australia, yellow-eye mullet are much more aggressive feeders and will take a much wider variety of baits, although they can be quite finicky, especially deep within estuaries. During winter on beaches or the mouths of estuaries, yellow-eye mullet readily take blue bait or whitebait as well as prawn, pipi, worms, maggots or small pieces of squid. Berley improves catches. Standard light surf rigs or double hook estuarine rigs works well. Yellow-eye mullet are often very close to shore, so long casts are not always necessary and the cast should be fished right to the shore. Yellow-eye mullet are good eating, especially fish which are taken from beaches or have not been grazing on algae.

Rigs and Tactics:

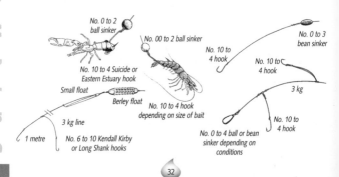

No. 0 to 2 ball sinker

No. 10 to 4 Suicide or Eastern Estuary hook

Small float

Berley float

3 kg line

1 metre

No. 6 to 10 Kendall Kirby or Long Shank hooks

No. 00 to 2 ball sinker

No. 10 to 4 hook depending on size of bait

No. 0 to 4 ball or bean sinker depending on conditions

No. 10 to 4 hook

No. 0 to 3 bean sinker

No. 10 to 4 hook

3 kg

No. 10 to 4 hook

Scientific name: *Lutjanus russelli*. Also known as One spot sea perch, finger-mark (WA).

Description: Has a general reddish or pinkish hue, a large mouth with discernible canine teeth and 14 or 15 rays in the dorsal fin. The Moses perch has a distinctive black spot which can be quite pale, below the start of the soft dorsal rays. Most of the black spot is above the obvious lateral line, while the similar black-spot sea perch (*Lutjanus fulviflamma*) has a small black spot, most of which is below the lateral line. The lateral yellow stripes of the black-spot sea perch are not present on the Moses perch.

The Moses perch often forms schools of similar sized fish, hanging near coral outcrops and in eddies near reefs. They can be found near drop-offs, on reefs or in depths of up to 80 m, with larger specimens frequently captured from deeper water. The Moses perch reaches 50 cm and nearly 3 kg but is commonly caught at between 25 and 30 centimetres.

Fishing: Like many species in this group, the Moses perch can be an aggressive feeder, rising well to minnow lures, feather jigs and even surface poppers cast or trolled to the downstream side of coral outcrops. The school can jostle to be the first to take the lure or bait.

Baits include whole or cut fish baits, squid, octopus or prawns. Weights should be kept to a minimum depending on the depth and mood of the fish, as Moses perch will rise to a bait which also puts them further from dangerous coral which they will try to use. In deeper water, lighter weights allow the fish to fight better and keeping the bait just above the bottom will deter some pickers .

The Moses perch is a good eating fish.

Rigs and Tactics:

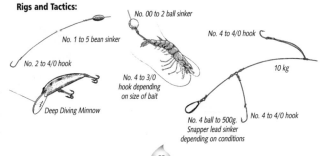

No. 1 to 5 bean sinker

No. 2 to 4/0 hook

Deep Diving Minnow

No. 00 to 2 ball sinker

No. 4 to 3/0 hook depending on size of bait

No. 4 to 4/0 hook

10 kg

No. 4 ball to 500g. Snapper lead sinker depending on conditions

No. 4 to 4/0 hook

QUEENFISH

Scientific name: *Scomberoides commersonnianus*. Also known as Giant leatherskin, leatherskin, queenie, talang queenfish, skinny, skinnyfish.

Description: The queenfish is a large and laterally (side to side) compressed species which leads to the common name of skinny and a light weight for the length. The mouth is large and extends well beyond the back of the eye whereas other smaller queenfish species have smaller mouths.

A series of 5 to 8 oval shaped blotches are found on the sides above the lateral line. The similar but smaller double spotted queenfish (*Scomberoides lysan*) has a double row of spots above and below the lateral line. The queenfish also has a prominent, high and light coloured front part of the dorsal and anal fins.

The queenfish can reach 120 cm and more than 11 kilograms. This light weight for the length indicates how skinny the queenfish is when viewed head on.

Fishing: Queenfish are found from the upper tidal reaches of tropical rivers to inshore reefs and occasionally near outer reefs which have shallow breaks. Queenfish prefer slightly turbid water with plenty of flow. They are ambush feeders and will lurk near cover such as eddies, rock bars, wharves and creek mouths, especially on a falling tide.

Queenfish are spectacular and exciting sportfish, with their slashing strikes and blistering runs, often with aerial displays. Queenfish will take dead baits such as mullet, pilchard, garfish, mudskippers, whiting or fresh prawns and squid. They are partial to live bait. Queenfish are renowned lure takers, with cast or trolled lures such as sliced chrome lures, spoons, shallow and deep diving minnows, and surface lures. Queenfish are excited by escaping baitfish, so a fast, erratic retrieve is most successful. Fly enthusiasts are increasingly targeting queenfish. Large minnow type flies retrieved through current eddies on a fast strip works best. A heavy monofilament leader is recommended when fishing for queenfish as their jaws and small teeth can damage light traces.

Rigs and Tactics:

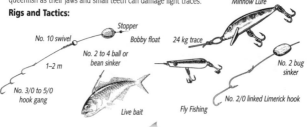

No. 10 swivel

Stopper

Bobby float

1–2 m

No. 2 to 4 ball or bean sinker

No. 3/0 to 5/0 hook gang

Live bait

Minnow Lure

24 kg trace

No. 2 bug sinker

Fly Fishing

No. 2/0 linked Limerick hook

SAILFISH, INDO-PACIFIC

Scientific name: *Istiophorus platypterus*. Also known as Pacific sailfish, bayonet fish, sailfish.

Description: The Indo-Pacific sailfish is most easily recognised by the prominent sail-like dorsal fin which when lowered, fits into a groove. The shorter median dorsal rays are still longer than the body is deep. The characteristic upper jaw spear is slender and more than twice the length of the lower jaw. The ventral rays are very long and extend almost to the anus. The body and sail are spotted with dark and light blue. Indo-Pacific sailfish can reach 120 kg, but any fish over 45 kg is a proud capture.

Fishing: The Indo-Pacific sailfish is a spectacular fish renowned for its spectacular leaps and strong surface runs. The sailfish is one of the smaller billfish but is highly prized, especially as a light line target. Sailfish can be taken by trolling live or dead baits of mullet, mackerel, garfish, rainbow runner or other common medium sized bait fish. Baits enhanced with plastic or feather skirts seem to take more fish. Many fish are taken on lures, including pusher or doorknob type lures or even minnow lures. Sailfish are becoming increasingly targeted with fly gear. Sailfish can travel in small pods and multiple hookups are possible, challenging the skills of all involved. The best sailfishing grounds are undoubtedly off Exmouth, Karratha and Broome in Western Australia, where even fairly small boats can encounter sailfish during peak periods.

Rigs and Tactics:

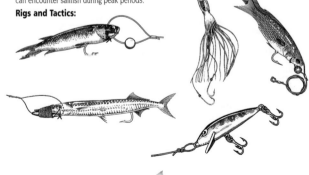

SAMSON FISH

Scientific name: *Seriola hippos*. Also known as Sambo, samson, sea kingfish.

Description: A common predator fish capable of reaching 1.8 m and more than 50 kg in weight. Similar in appearance to the closely related yellowtail kingfish, but the samson fish is a much cleaner fighter which does not usually bury the angler. The samson fish is best separated by second dorsal rays which has 23 – 25 as opposed to 31 or over for yellowtail kingfish. The 16 – 17 anal rays on the samson fish distinguish this species from the amberjack which has 19 or more anal rays and 29 to 35 second dorsal rays. The samson fish also has a more rounded forehead.

The flesh surrounding the teeth in both jaws in the samson fish is often but not always engorged with blood, giving the tooth patches a red appearance. The colour varies but the samson fish can often have distinct vertical blotches which, while fading with age, are not found in the other similar species.

Fishing: A real challenge on light gear as skillful handling can present some extremely large fish due to their relatively clean, strong fight. Samson fish can be taken at all depths from nearshore waters to around 30 fathoms. They can be found near sand patches, around reefs or seagrass and can take whiting, garfish or other small fish from surprised anglers. Samson fish can be taken on deep vertical fished jigs with aggregations near Rottnest attracting international interest from October to February. Tagged fish have moved from Rottnest to Albany in 21 days! Small samson fish make good eating.

Rigs and Tactics:

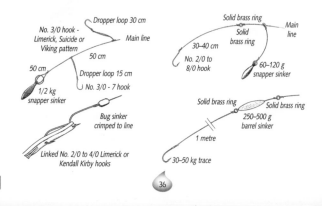

SALMON, AUSTRALIAN

Scientific name: *Arripis truttucca*. Also known as Salmon, black back, cocky salmon, colonial salmon, kahawai. Salmon trout and bay trout, (juveniles).

Description: The 'salmon' is not related to true trout and salmon in the family Salmonidae and are more closely related to the mullets. Australian salmon reaches 9 kg.

The forked tail of adult salmon is dark, and the eye is generally yellow. The body is classically torpedo shaped and full of power. The head, and the mouth are moderately large. There are distinctive brown dots or dashes along the dorsal surface although the larger specimens become dark across the back. The belly is silvery to white. The Australian salmon moves along the south coast in summer and up the west coast reaching Perth in small numbers around Easter.

Fishing: The Australian salmon is one of the best light tackle sportsfish in Australia. They are the best fighting fish taken from the beach, where their strong runs and spectacular leaps more than compensate for the average eating quality.

Australian salmon form large schools making them vulnerable to commercial fishing. There is little doubt that commercial fishing can affect local abundance and recreational fishing quality. These schools can provide spectacular fishing, but on occasions these schooling fish will not feed. Australian salmon are frequently caught on pilchards and cut baits, with belly fillets or baits with white skin attached doing better. Pipis, cockles and beach worms work and can surprise whiting fisherman. In estuaries, salmon trout are often taken on whitebait, blue bait, prawns or squid. The bite of the salmon is frequently quite fumbling and some patience is required before setting the hook.

Rigs and Tactics:

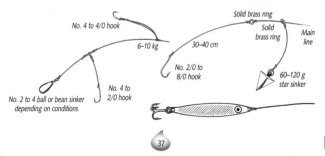

SALMON, THREADFIN

Scientific name: *Polydactylus sheridani*. Also known as Blue threadfin, blue salmon, Burnett salmon, king salmon.

Description: The threadfin salmon is similar to the Cooktown salmon, but possesses 5 long, distinctive fingers on the lower edge of the pectoral fin. This species has a more pronounced blue colour and a long and relatively narrow caudal wrist. The threadfin salmon is common between 0.5 and around 3 kg with occasional specimens slightly larger.

Another similar species, the Northern or striped threadfin salmon (*Polydactylus plebius*) is separated by its more prominent stripes and overall golden colour and five free filaments, of which the two uppermost are longest.

Rigs and Tactics:

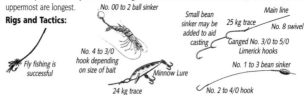

No. 00 to 2 ball sinker

Small bean sinker may be added to aid casting

25 kg trace

Main line

No. 8 swivel

Ganged No. 3/0 to 5/0 Limerick hooks

Fly fishing is successful

No. 4 to 3/0 hook depending on size of bait

Minnow Lure

24 kg trace

No. 1 to 3 bean sinker

No. 2 to 4/0 hook

SNOOK

Scientific name: *Sphyraena novaehollandiae*. Also known as Short finned sea pike, sea pike, short finned barracuda.

Description: It is easily separated from the barracuda by its southern range and the first dorsal fin which commences well behind the end of the pectoral fin. The snook is similar to the long finned sea pike but most easily separated by the snook's shorter anal fin, and its ventral fins which are set well behind the pectoral fin. The snook reaches 1.1 m and 5 kilograms and is a highly regarded sportfish. It is often trolled with chrome lures over inshore weed beds.

SHARK, TIGER

Scientific name: *Galeocerdo cuvier.*

Description: A large and extremely dangerous species of shark. The tiger shark can be found well offshore and can venture into the surf zone on occasions, especially during breeding season. The characteristic colour pattern of the tiger shark is a tiger-like series of bars on the upper body. The teeth are unusually shaped, being large and pointed backwards, with strong serrations, especially on the back edge. Although the colouring and shape are distinctive, a dive charter at Ningaloo Reef, with a boat load of tourists, attempted to dive with a tiger shark they thought was a whale shark. The shark, like many when well fed and not threatened, was docile and there was no real incident.

The tiger shark can reach nearly 6.5 m and more than 600 kilograms.

Fishing: The tiger shark is a famous visitor to the old whaling stations of Australia, where large numbers of tigers, would attack whale carcasses waiting to be flensed.

Tiger sharks are attracted by berley and are taken with very large dead baits, especially those with oily or bloody flesh. The tiger shark is a powerful and dogged opponent and is sought by some specialist gamefishermen. Taking any large shark from small boats requires enormous preparation and should not be attempted by any inexperienced angler.

The tiger shark is a large and opportunistic feeder which will attack humans and should be treated with extreme caution. If sharks are not being targeted and a large tiger shark shows up – move.

Rigs and Tactics:

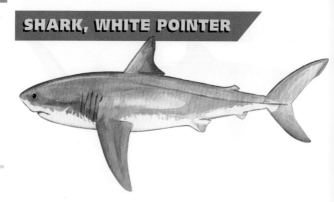

Scientific name: *Carcharodon carcharias*. Also known as Great white shark, white shark, white death.

Description: The white pointer shark is a large and extremely dangerous species and the star of the Jaws movies which has lead to the misguided destruction of many harmless sharks. However, the white pointer is responsible for more attacks on humans than any other species. The white pointer, reaches 6.4 m and more than 1200 kilograms. As in most shark species, males are smaller and easily identified by the claspers which assist in copulation.

The white pointer shark has a conical snout, long gill slits and extremely sharp, serrated triangular teeth. The colour is generally grey to dark grey above with a white belly.

The white pointer prefers oceanic waters and does not often move close inshore, except to breed or to follow seal colonies when pups are produced. They are more commonly found inshore along the south coast but have been observed off Perth beaches in recent years. There is much more danger involved in driving to the beach than from a shark while swimming, but the white death evokes a primitive fear in many, many people.

Fishing: The white pointer is now totally protected. There are special procedures for the few fish which are hooked by recreational fishers.

White pointers were viewed as the ultimate capture for game fishermen, with many young recreational fishers being aware of Bob Dyer's 1062 kg fish from Moreton Island and Alf Dean's 1208 kg fish in 1960 from South Australia.

Rigs and Tactics: Not applicable as White Pointer Shark are a protected species.

SNAPPER

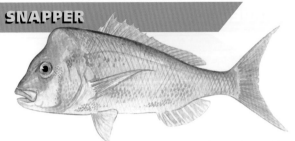

Scientific name: *Pagrus auratus.* (formerly *Chrysophrys auratus*) Also known as schnapper, Pink snapper and pinkie.

Description: A truly stunning and highly sought after species, the snapper can have iridescent pink to burnished copper colouration with bright blue spots from the lateral line upwards which are brightest in younger fish. A hump on the head and nose area develops in some fish and is more likely in male fish. Snapper are relatively slow growing and mature at 29 to 35 cm and four to five years of age. Snapper numbers have been affected by both commercial and recreational overfishing but have recovered well in Shark Bay with good management.

Fishing: Snapper are traditionally taken on bottom paternoster rigs. Snapper prefer the edges of reefs or broken ground and can be taken from the shore or as deep as 100 fathoms. Drifting over broken ground or drop-offs at the edges of reefs with just enough weight to bounce bottom will find fish and repeated drifts will pick up more fish. Snapper form schools of similar sized fish, with the size of the school decreasing with larger fish.

Snapper are a magnificent fighting fish and are excellent eating, but do not freeze particularly well.

There are special rules in WA to protect spawning aggregations of snapper so check the rules, fish to 15 kilograms can still be regularly taken from Cockburn Sound near Perth.

Rigs and Tactics:

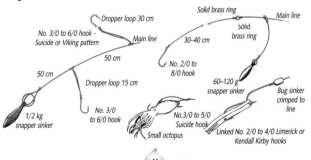

SNAPPER, QUEEN

Scientific name: *Nemadactylus valenciennesi*. Also known as southern blue morwong

Description: A handsome representative of the morwong family, the queen snapper is often a rich blue colour. There are distinctive yellow lines on the face and around the eyes and there is usually a large black blotch in the middle of the side of the fish. The queen snapper has the extended rays of the pectoral fin like many of the morwongs. The tail fin is deeply forked.

The queen snapper is found from southern reefs to a depth of 240 m and has a preference for reef country.

SNAPPER, RED

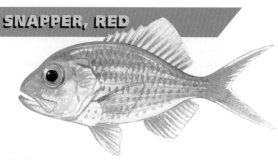

Scientific name: *Centroberyx gerrardi*. Also known as Bight redfish.

Description: The red snapper is most commonly a species of deeper reefs in cooler southern waters which may range from shallow reefs to more than 300 metres. Very similar to the smaller nannygai but is able to be separated by having 6 dorsal fin spines versus 7 in the nannygai.

The red snapper has a distinctive white line along the lateral line and white margins on the fins. The head is also less rounded than in the nannygai. The eye is generally red but can fade to red-silver after death. The red snapper can reach 66 cm, but is more common at 40 – 45 centimetres. It is found singly in larger sizes or in small groups when smaller and is taken with standard reef rigs and baits.

TAILOR

Scientific name: *Pomatomus saltatrix*. Also known as Tailer, chopper, bluefish (USA), elf (South Africa), skipjack.

Description: The tailor is best known for its relatively small but extremely sharp teeth. The tailor has a moderately forked tail, and a bluish to blue-green back which changes to more silvery and white on the belly. The eye can be yellow. The fins vary in colour but the tail fin is usually darker than the others.

Juvenile tailor are found in estuaries and embayments. Larger tailor move to the beaches and inshore reefs at between 25 – 35 centimetres. Tailor can reach 10 kg with any fish over 5 kg being rightly claimed as a prize and fish over 1.5 kg being large. Tailor are voracious feeders, with individual fish gorging themselves before regurgitating to continue in a feeding frenzy.

Fishing: Tailor are a highly prized species which readily takes a bait, fights hard and, if bled immediately after capture make fine eating. Tailor can be taken from boat or shore, on lure, fly or bait and by anglers of any skill level. A fast retrieved popper through white water works well.

The most common bait and rig would be a whole pilchard bait on a gang hook rig. In the surf and where casting distance is required, a sliding sinker rig works best, or with a star or spoon sinker on a dropper trace. In estuaries, from a boat, or in calmer surf, an unweighted or minimally weighted bait provides by far the best results. Tailor readily feed high in the water column and avidly attack a floating bait. Tailor bite best at dusk and dawn. Huge tailor are regularly taken in Shark Bay.

Tailor makes a quality cut bait.

Rigs and Tactics:

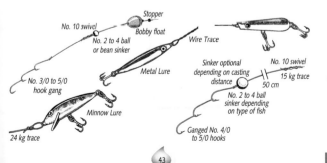

TARWHINE

Scientific name: *Rhabdosargus sarba*. Also known as Silver bream.

Description: The tarwhine is similar to the various bream species but has a number of thin golden or brown stripes running the length of the otherwise silver body. The nose of the tarwhine is blunt and there are 11 or 12 anal rays whereas bream have 9 or fewer. The fins other than the dorsal fin are generally bright yellow or yellow-orange and the tarwhine has a black lining to its gut cavity. Tarwhine are common in inshore and estuarine areas and may be found on offshore reefs on occasions. Tarwhine form schools, especially in smaller sizes. Tarwhine can reach 80 cm and more than 3 kg but they are most commonly caught at a few hundred grams.

Fishing: Tarwhine can be voracious feeders, taking a wide variety of foods. Tarwhine readily take cut flesh, bluebait, whitebait and parts of pilchard but many are caught on prawn, pipi, worm, or squid baits.

While tarwhine bite very hard, their relatively small mouth and frequent small size makes them nuisance bait pickers in many instances. In estuaries or shallow waters, a light running ball sinker rig works best while off the rocks or in deeper water, use as little weight and as light a rig as you can get away with. Tarwhine fight well for their size. They also make very good eating although they can have an iodine taste if not bled immediately and the guts and black stomach lining removed as soon as possible.

Rigs and Tactics:

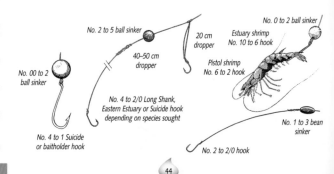

No. 00 to 2 ball sinker

No. 4 to 1 Suicide or baitholder hook

No. 2 to 5 ball sinker

40–50 cm dropper

No. 4 to 2/0 Long Shank, Eastern Estuary or Suicide hook depending on species sought

20 cm dropper

No. 2 to 2/0 hook

No. 0 to 2 ball sinker

Estuary shrimp
No. 10 to 6 hook

Pistol shrimp
No. 6 to 2 hook

No. 1 to 3 bean sinker

TOADFISH, WEEPING

Scientific name: *Torquigener pleurogramma*. Also known as blowie, common blowfish.

Description: This is a fairly small species only reaching 22 cm and commonly found in sandy surf areas and around jetties and pylons where they are many children's first fish.

The diagnostic feature is the single dark brown stripe down the side and up to six narrow dark bands which run downwards across the cheek and near the eye, giving the appearance of tear stains.

Like all toadfish, the banded toadfish can inflate its abdomen with air or water and small rough spikelets are extended.

Fishing: The weeping toadfish, in common with the other similar toadfish species can be caught on a variety of small baits, which can fit into the small mouth with its sharp fused teeth. This species can occur in plague proportions in many estuaries and are widely despised.

They should never be kept and consumed or fed to domestic pets as there have been a number of fatalities, including humans. The toxins are strongest in the skin and internal organs, especially the liver.

Rigs and Tactics: Not applicable as Toadfish are not recommended as an angling species.

TREVALLY, BIGEYE

Scientific name: *Caranx sexfasciatus*. Also known as Great trevally.

Description: The bigeye trevally is best identified by the gelatinous covering to the rear of the relatively large eye. There are white tips to the dorsal and anal fins and a small black spot on the rear edge of the gill cover. The bigeye trevally's breast is fully scaled. The soft dorsal fin of the bigeye trevally has 19 – 22 soft rays while the turrum, has 25 – 30 rays.

Larger fish patrol close to deep drop-offs especially those close to high tidal flows or near reef gaps. This is not a large species, reaching only 80 centimetres.

Fishing: An avid lure taker, the bigeye trevally is fished near areas of fast water near reef gaps on the outgoing tide. Poppers work extremely well, with chrome slices, minnow lures and jigs also appealing to these strong fighters. On a rising tide, these fish can often be on the inside of the reef edges or areas where break-offs are more common. Bigeye trevally readily take small live baits. The removal of the red meat along the lateral line will make the taste more mild.

TREVALLY, GOLDEN

Scientific name: *Gnathanodon speciosus*.

Description: The golden trevally is a large species reaching 1.2 m and 37 kilograms.

Juvenile golden trevally are striking and are often associated with large fish or sharks. They are a bright gold with vertical black stripes the first of which passes through the eye.

Larger fish lose the distinctive stripes and the eye is quite small. These fish are often quite silvery when caught but flash yellow as they die and then are golden coloured, especially on the belly. A number of black spots are often present on the side, commonly near the tail but the number and size varies and they may not be present. The most obvious feature of this species is that they lack teeth. Very good eating.

Fishing: Like many trevally, golden trevally form schools of similar sized fish, with smaller schools of larger fish. Large golden trevally are often taken trolling minnow lures in the vicinity of offshore reefs.

Smaller fish are taken by shore based or small boat anglers either with lures including poppers, slices, spoons or minnow lures or less commonly on fly.

Golden trevally take baits well, with prawns, pilchard, small fish or cut baits working well. Over sand, the baits can be weighted, but near reefs, lightly weighted or floating baits work better as the further any trevally moves from a reef to take a bait, the better the chances of landing it, as they fight very strongly and make use of any rocky outcrop.

Golden trevally make very good eating, especially if bled and chilled immediately on capture.

Rigs and Tactics:

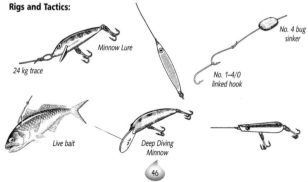

24 kg trace

Minnow Lure

No. 4 bug sinker

No. 1–4/0 linked hook

Live bait

Deep Diving Minnow

TREVALLY, GIANT

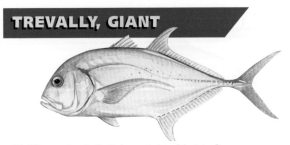

Scientific name: *Caranx ignobilis.* Also known as Lowly trevally, barrier trevally.

Description: The giant trevally is the largest trevally reaching 1.7 m in length and 60 kg which would be almost unstoppable on stand up fishing tackle. The steep profile of the head is typical of the giant trevally. There is also a small scale-less area on the ventral surface immediately in front of the ventral fins. A small patch of scales is generally found in the middle of this otherwise scale-less patch. There is no opercular (cheek) spot which is present on the bigeye trevally.

As giant trevally increase in size, they form smaller schools with the largest fish frequently loners. Large fish also prefer deeper channels between large reefs while smaller fish are found on tidal flats or on the edges of shallower reefs.

Fishing: Small giant trevally are one of the most challenging species for lure fishers in the tropics, with spinning near the edges of reefs, on drop-offs on tidal flats or sight fishing to individuals or small schools working well. Poppers are particularly attractive to these fish and can also be used as a teaser for fly fishers. Giant trevally also take minnow lures, large spoons and lead-headed jigs.

Rigs and Tactics:

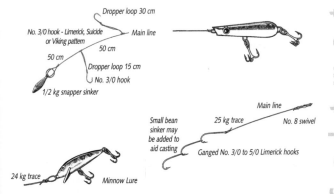

Dropper loop 30 cm

No. 3/0 hook - Limerick, Suicide or Viking pattern

Main line

50 cm

50 cm

Dropper loop 15 cm

No. 3/0 hook

1/2 kg snapper sinker

Main line

Small bean sinker may be added to aid casting

25 kg trace

No. 8 swivel

Ganged No. 3/0 to 5/0 Limerick hooks

24 kg trace

Minnow Lure

saltwater Species

TREVALLY, SILVER

Scientific name: *Pseudocaranx dentex*. Also known as White trevally, skipjack trevally, skippy.

Description: A common schooling fish to cooler waters, the silver trevally is found in inshore areas but may be found offshore. Juveniles are often encountered in estuaries and bays but larger fish can also be found in these areas on occasions. The fins may be yellow and a narrow yellow stripe is often found on these fish but most fish are silver with a blue-green or darker blue, and dark bands may be present. The silver trevally can reach 1 m and more but fish to 2 kg are much more common and in most areas a fish of 3 kg is noteworthy. The mouth is relatively small, finishing well in front of the start of the eye and the lips are rubbery. There is an obvious black spot on the rear edge of the opercular (cheek) bone.

Fishing: Like all trevally, they can be good sport, especially on light line. Silver trevally can be taken on small lures such as small spoons, leadhead jigs and small minnow lures. While silver trevally can feed on the surface, they prefer to feed on or near sandy or gravel bottoms, taking baits such as half pilchard, bluebait, whitebait, cut fish baits, squid or prawn, depending on the food found in the area fished. Silver trevally respond well to berley.

Silver trevally can be taken on lines of 3 – 8 kg where they provide excellent sport. As they are a schooling fish which are not too prone to disperse if one fish escapes, persistence pays off with light line. Silver trevally are fair eating, and must be bled on capture.

Rigs and Tactics:

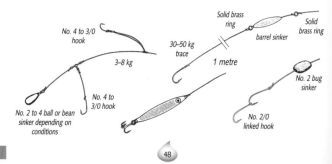

TROUT, BAR CHEEKED CORAL

Scientific name: P*lectropomus maculatus*. Also known as Bar-cheeked trout, coral cod.

Range: Abrolhos Islands in Western Australia and tropical waters.

Description: The bar-cheeked coral trout can be as brilliantly coloured as the coral trout with which it is often confused. The bar-cheek coral trout is most easily separated by the blue spots on the head being elongated and not round as they are in coral trout. This species is smaller than the coral trout, reaching 70 cm and 6 kg but can be susceptible to overfishing and is generally taken at a smaller size. Almost all coral trout taken in WA are this species.

The bar-cheek coral trout has the same powerful tail which is used to good effect to bury anglers in reef country. It has a large mouth and sharp but widely spaced canine teeth.

Fishing: One of the premier reef fish due to its brilliant appearance, hard fight near coral outcrops and excellent eating. The bar-cheek coral trout can be taken on bait, lure and fly. Trolled minnow lures and cast poppers, slices or jigs put near coral outcrops or channels between reefs can provide exciting sport.

The proximity of sharp coral outcrops in many locations means that if the fish is given his head a break-off is certain. Quality tackle and close attention, especially when trolling is required. The larger fish can be taken in deeper water. The bar-cheek coral trout can take large baits. Best baits are live baits, with whole fish and fresh fillets working well, and squid, prawn and crab taking fish. A trace can offer some protection during the fight. This species makes excellent eating.

Rigs and Tactics:

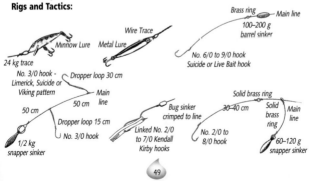

TROUT, CORONATION

Scientific name: *Variola louti*. Also known as Lunar-tailed cod, fairy cod.

Range: Shark Bay in Western Australia and around the top end.

Description: The coronation trout is a beautiful fish which has vivid red or red-orange colouration flecked with yellow or red. The tail is distinctive with a sickle or lunar crescent shape and a distinctive yellow trailing edge. The cheeks and all the other fins are tinged with yellow on the trailing edge.

The coronation trout is quite common on coral reefs, but may be found on deeper reefs to 100 metres. It grows to 80 cm and around 3 kilograms.

Fishing: The coronation trout shares many features from an angling perspective with the coral trout, including a large mouth, aggressive nature, a strong lure taker and excellent eating. They can have tapeworms in the guts which do not affect the eating quality of the fish.

Coronation trout can be taken on minnows, jigs and chrome lures and flies. Live baits, dead baits and cut baits work best. A trace is an advantage, especially as coral trout can be taken from the same areas. As the coronation trout will move upwards to take a bait, less weight is necessary and a mobile approach, casting or drifting with the tide on reef edges or channels works well. The fight is strong, but the fish are not as big as coral trout.

Rigs and Tactics:

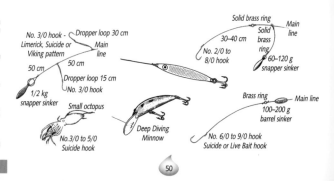

50

TRUMPETER, STRIPED

Scientific name: *Pelates sexlineatus*. Also known as Striped perch, striped grunter, trump.

Description: A small species reaching 32 cm and around 500 g, but more common at a bait stealing 25 centimetres. The striped trumpeter forms schools in coastal bays and estuaries over sand or weed bottom or near broken ground.

The small mouth makes hooking difficult. The short head is quite rounded and there are around 5 – 6 lines running through the head and along the body. There may be a number of vertical blotches with one most prominent behind the head overlaying the stripes. The top stripes may be wavy.

Fishing: While frequently considered a pest species, the striped trumpeter is a frequent early encounter for young anglers. The striped trumpeter will take most baits, but the small mouth means that a small long-shanked hook will improve catches. Baits of peeled prawns, cut flesh, blue bait, pipi, worms, or squid work well, with more robust baits such as squid recommended. Striped trumpeter make hardy and quality live baits.

Striped trumpeter are not highly regarded as food fish but are often served to the family by proud young fishermen.

Rigs and Tactics:

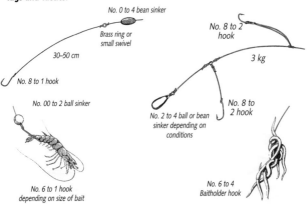

No. 0 to 4 bean sinker

Brass ring or small swivel

30–50 cm

No. 8 to 1 hook

No. 8 to 2 hook

3 kg

No. 2 to 4 ball or bean sinker depending on conditions

No. 8 to 2 hook

No. 00 to 2 ball sinker

No. 6 to 1 hook depending on size of bait

No. 6 to 4 Baitholder hook

saltwater species

TUNA, LONGTAIL

Scientific name: *Thunnus tonggol*. Also known as Northern bluefin tuna, northern blue.

Description: The name longtail comes from the light build to the rear half of this species, giving a narrow tail wrist and a slender outline. The pectoral fin is very short and finishes well in front of the start of the second dorsal fin which readily separates the species from yellowfin and bigeye tuna. This species is much more common in tropical waters but can migrate southwards in summer.

Fishing: In tropical waters, small longtails can form vast schools like mackerel tuna or bonito. These schools move rapidly and fish can be caught by casting lures or trolling lures or baits near the edge of the feeding school. Minnow lures, lead slugs or Christmas tree lures, feather jigs, spoons and flies all work well with larger fish preferring larger lures and a faster retrieve.

Longtail prefer inshore waters and although most are taken by anglers in boats, longtail are a highly prized land based game species. Specialised gear with live baits below large floats or balloons or high speed spinning can bring these speedsters to the rocks at places like Steep Point.

Longtail love live baits fished from boats and cubing (berleying with tuna flesh and feeding unweighted cubes into the trail, (one with a hook) can work well.

Longtail tuna are red fleshed and of lower quality than many species, but it is greatly improved with immediate bleeding.

Rigs and Tactics

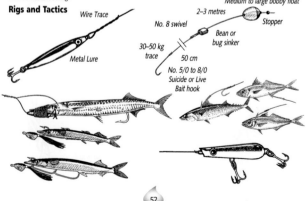

TUNA, MACKEREL

Scientific name: *Euthynnus affinis*. Also known as Jack mackerel, little tuna, kawa-kawa.

Description: The mackerel tuna is a highly prized lightweight game species which is caught in inshore waters or larger bays, harbours as well as around offshore islands or larger reefs. The mackerel tuna can reach 1 m in length and 12 kg but is much more common at 2 – 8 kilograms.

The mackerel tuna has prominent wavy green lines in the rear portion of the body above the midline. The mackerel tuna is similar to the frigate mackerel but the first dorsal of the mackerel tuna reaches almost to the second dorsal while the frigate mackerel's first dorsal is widely separated from the second dorsal fin. The mackerel tuna has two to five dark spots above the ventral fin, prominent teeth and reaches 58 cm in length.

Fishing: The mackerel tuna is a schooling fish which feeds heavily on pilchards, herrings, whitebait, anchovies, squid and occasionally krill. However, even when a feeding school is located, they can be very selective and difficult to entice to strike.

Mackerel tuna are mainly taken on fast trolled or high speed retrieved lures such as plastic skirted lures, Christmas tree lures, minnow lures, plastic squids, lead jigs and feather lures and spoons. The mackerel tuna will take live baits, fresh dead baits either cast and retrieved, trolled or fished under a float. They will more rarely take cut baits.

Rigs and Tactics:

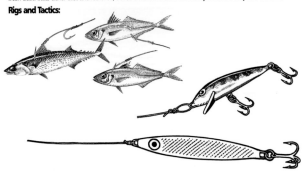

TUNA, SOUTHERN BLUEFIN

Scientific name: *Thunnus maccoyii*. Also known as SBT, southern blue, bluefin, bluey, tunny.

Description: The southern bluefin tuna is a heavily built and very highly prized species which prefers open oceanic waters, especially in larger sizes. The southern bluefin tuna can grow to greater than 150 kg. In WA small southern bluefin can be found in inshore waters and weigh from 3 – 25 kg, with the average size increasing as you move eastwards along the southern coast.

Southern bluefin tuna have been overexploited by commercial fishing operations. Southern bluefin tuna can be identified by their heavy bodies, and the short pectoral fins which do not extend to the second dorsal. The dorsal and anal fins are also short as opposed to the yellowfin with its scythe-like lobes in larger fish. The finlets at the rear of the body are edged with black and the caudal keels on the wrist of the tail are conspicuously yellow, especially in the sizes normally encountered by recreational fishers.

Fishing: Most southern bluefin tuna are taken on trolled lures, with rubber squids, pushers and other gamefishing lures working well. They will also take minnow lures, feathers, slices and large lead slugs. Southern bluefin tuna like offshore debris and can be taken around floating logs, shipping containers or other large flotsam in bluewater areas.

Southern bluefin tuna are less frequently taken on baits, although they can be taken on trolled baits, live baits or dead baits including cubes, especially if used with berley. Deep fished live baits or whole squid can take larger fish, but local knowledge is necessary.

The southern bluefin tuna has rich dark meat which is highly prized for sashimi.

TUNA, STRIPED

Scientific name: *Katsuwonis pelamis*. Also known as Skipjack, skipjack tuna, stripey, aku.

Description: The striped tuna is a small, thickset schooling species which rapidly tapers at the rear of the body to a smallish tail. Sometimes misidentified as a bonito, but striped tuna lack the obvious teeth of the bonito and have no stripes on the upper flanks or back. The 4 – 6 horizontal stripes on the striped tuna are found on the lower flanks and belly. The area under and around the pectoral fin lacks stripes.

The striped tuna can reach more than 15 kg, but in Australia any fish over 10 kg is exceptional and the average size is between 1 and 6 kilograms. Schools of striped tuna can be massive and may contain hundreds of tonnes of fish. Average eating but good fun on lures..

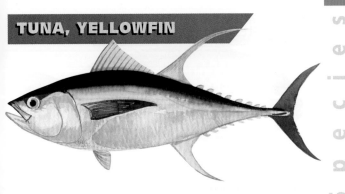

Scientific name: *Thunnus albacares.* Also known as Allison tuna, yellowfin or 'fin, ahi.

Description: The yellowfin tuna is a beautiful, powerful and challenging species which prefers warmer currents but may move inshore where deep water comes close to the coast. The yellowfin tuna is easily separated from other tunas by the scythe-like dorsal and anal lobes in adult fish. The pectoral fin is long and extends to the commencement of the second dorsal fin.

Small yellowfin have short dorsal and anal lobes, but have whitish bars down the sides which may disappear after death. The liver of yellowfin tuna is smooth as opposed to the ridged liver of the bigeye. The caudal keels (ridges) on the wrist of the tail are also dusky and never yellow as in the southern bluefin tuna.

Yellowfin tuna can reach more than 200 kg in other parts of the world, but in Australia fish over 100 kg are magnificent and most fish are between 2 and 50 kilograms. They are excellent eating.

Rigs and Tactics:

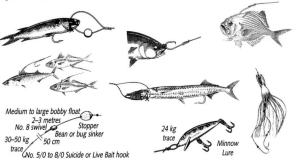

Medium to large bobby float,
2–3 metres
No. 8 swivel   Stopper
30–50 kg   Bean or bug sinker
trace   50 cm
No. 5/0 to 8/0 Suicide or Live Bait hook

24 kg
trace   Minnow
Lure

Saltwater Species

TUSKFISH, BLACK SPOT

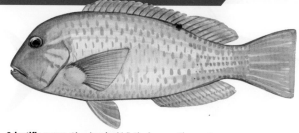

Scientific name: *Choerodon schoenleinii*. Also known as Blue parrot.

Range: Point Quobba northwards and tropical waters.

Description: A large tuskfish capable of reaching 15 kg and is found in sand and weed areas adjacent to coral reefs. The black-spot tuskfish is easily identified by the black spot which is found at the base of the middle of the dorsal fin. There is often a short, oblique purple bar set behind the eye and the tail is generally bright purple. The overall body colour is generally blue and the chin is blue-green or purple whereas in the blue tuskfish (*Choerodon cyanodus*) which is a smaller species, the chin is white or off-white.

Fishing: The black-spot tuskfish has a strong preference for crab baits but can be taken on prawns, squid, pipi and worms. The black-spot tusk fish can often be observed and cast to, making presentation with lightly weighted baits less difficult, but they can be difficult to entice to strike on occasion. Because this species can move close inshore to graze on corals in a quest for larger food, they can be taken by spearfishermen.

The black-spot tuskfish can be caught near deeper reefs and larger specimens are more likely. The black-spot tuskfish can be a challenging capture as they can cut off the unwary on nearby coral outcrops and is not easily brought to the boat. The black-spot tuskfish is excellent eating with firm white flesh.

Rigs and Tactics:

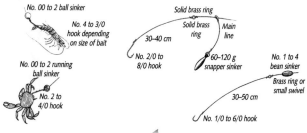

No. 00 to 2 ball sinker

No. 4 to 3/0 hook depending on size of bait

No. 00 to 2 running ball sinker

No. 2 to 4/0 hook

Solid brass ring

Solid brass ring

Main line

30–40 cm

No. 2/0 to 8/0 hook

60–120 g snapper sinker

No. 1 to 4 bean sinker

Brass ring or small swivel

30–50 cm

No. 1/0 to 6/0 hook

Scientific name: *Sillaginodes punctata.* Also known as Spotted whiting, KG, KGW.

Description: The King George whiting is the largest and most sought after whiting species in Australia reaching 67 cm and more than 2 kg, with the largest specimens found in oceanic waters. Juveniles spend time near sea grass beds inshore or in estuaries before moving to more open waters. King George whiting prefer sand patches near weed beds, gravel or broken reef country. King George whiting are readily identified by the distinctive dark brown or red-brown spots and broken dashes along the body.

Fishing: The King George whiting is a magnificent and hard fighting whiting species. Smaller fish succumb most readily to baits of prawn, pipi, mussel, and worms. These baits are fished on light line with minimal weight near the edges of drop-offs or sand patches in sea grass beds or reef areas. Larger fish are often caught on blue sardines or whitebait. The largest King George whiting are taken on reef fishing rigs near reefs in depths up to 30 metres.

The best King George whiting experts adopt a mobile approach, fishing sand patches near heavy cover and moving on if there are no bites in a few minutes. The King George whiting is magnificent eating, combining the meat quality of all whiting in a size large enough that generous boneless fillets can be obtained.

Rigs and Tactics:

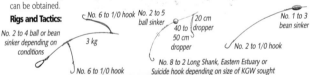

No. 2 to 4 ball or bean sinker depending on conditions — 3 kg — No. 6 to 1/0 hook

No. 6 to 1/0 hook — No. 2 to 5 ball sinker — 40 to 50 cm dropper / 20 cm dropper — No. 8 to 2 Long Shank, Eastern Estuary or Suicide hook depending on size of KGW sought

No. 1 to 3 bean sinker — No. 2 to 1/0 hook

Scientific name: *Sillago maculata.* Also known as Diver whiting, winter whiting, spotted whiting.

Description: The trumpeter whiting is a common schooling fish with a preference for silty bottom or deeper gutters of bays and estuaries. The trumpeter whiting is more commonly taken during the cooler months. The trumpeter whiting reaches 30 centimetres.

It is easily identified by having a series of irregular and disjointed brown blotches, spots or vertical marks. The similar southern school whiting (*Sillago bassensis*) has unbroken vertical stripes. Both species have a silver stripe along the middle of the body. Excellent eating.

saltwater species

WHITING, YELLOWFIN

Scientific name: *Sillago schomburgkii* Also known as western sand whiting, yellow-finned whiting

Description: A similar species to the sand whiting but lacks the black spot at the base of the pectoral fin. The characteristic yellow to orange ventral and anal fins become less apparent in larger individuals. There is no obvious silver strip along the sides or any markings on the dorsal surface.

It is found in estuaries and surf areas and can reach 42 centimetres. It is not uncommon at around 33 – 35 centimetres.

Fishing: The excellent eating which this species provides makes it a worthwhile target for anglers. While they may be found in the estuaries, with the exception of the Peel-Harvey estuary, the best specimens are taken from ocean beaches. A light ball sinker and a bluebait or whitebait on small ganged hooks fished on a flick rod are highly recommended. When fishing for whiting, fishing at your feet first is good advice as many anglers cast way out behind the active feeding zone of this fish. They fish much better on a rising tide and can be in the sand wash area in only a few centimetres of water. A slow retrieve works best.

Rigs and Tactics:

No. 1 to 3 bean sinker

No. 8 to 4 long shank hook

bug sinker

No. 6 to 2 linked Limerick hook

No. 00 to 1 ball sinker

No. 6 to 4 light gauge fly hook

WAHOO

Scientific name: *Acanthocybium solandri*. Also known as Ono, 'hoo.

Description: The wahoo is capable of very fast movement in the water. Most wahoo in Australian waters are between 8 and 30 kg but they can reach 65 kilograms.

The wahoo is an open water species which can be identified by the long and higher dorsal fin of approximately even height. The dorsal fin starts behind the front of the pectoral fin while with the Spanish mackerel it commences at the leading edge of the pectoral. The head is longer and more pointed with the wahoo and the trailing edge of the tail fin is vertical.

The wahoo has a number of prominent zebra-like vertical stripes. Has very sharp teeth and can badly damage or cut off very expensive marlin lures.

Scientific name: *Hephaestus fuliginosus*. Also known as Black bream, purple grunter, sooty.

Description: In the wild, sooty grunter can reach 4 kg and 50 cm. This species has a reasonably large mouth and the lips may be blubbery in some specimens. Colour can be extremely variable, from light brown to black. Sooty grunter can be omnivorous and will on occasion eat green algae.

Fishing: The sooty grunter prefers faster water in rivers and can inhabit mid-stream snags in riffles. In dams these fish are found around cover, especially fallen timber. Sooty grunter will readily take live shrimp or cherabin, worms or grubs. They will take a variety of lures including diving lures, spinner baits, bladed spinners, jigs, soft plastics and flies. Sooty grunter fight well without jumping and are undervalued as a sport fish by many anglers, partly because they are reasonably common in many areas.

Sooty grunter are a fair to poor food fish which can be weedy tasting. Species such as barramundi which occur in the same areas are much better fare.

Rigs and Tactics:

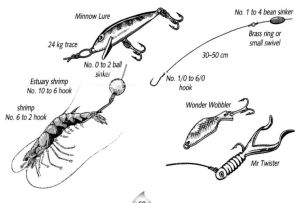

Freshwater Species

REDFIN

Scientific name: *Perca fluviatilis*. Also known as English perch, European perch, redfin perch, reddie.

Description: The redfin has prominent scales and five to six prominent vertical stripes which may extend nearly to the belly. These stripes are less prominent in larger fish. The dorsal fin is set well forward and when erect, resembles a small 'sail'. The ventral and anal fins are often very bright red or orange, often with a tinge of white at the ends. The tail fin can also be bright orange, or orange-yellow.

Redfin are often found schooling around drowned timber, at drop-offs near points, or on submerged islands. Redfin prefer cooler water and in summer, the largest fish are almost always below the thermocline in dams or large river holes. Redfin are aggressive and prolific breeders. In impoundments they can stunt out, producing thousands of mature fish as small as 15 cm. In other areas, they can reach 3 kg and provide excellent sport with a variety of techniques.

Fishing: In dams, anchor among drowned timber and bob with bait or lures. A small ball sinker runs to the top of the hook which is baited with worm, cricket, grub or shrimp. The bait is lowered to the bottom and vertically jigged between 30 cm and a metre or so before being dropped to the bottom. Lure casting near drowned timber in large holes in rivers or near drop-offs in rivers or dams is very succesful. Bladed, Celta type lures, diving lures, jigs and small Rapala minnows taking many fish. In WA southern fresh water redfin are the common target species and are a top class sport and feed fish.

Rigs and Tactics:

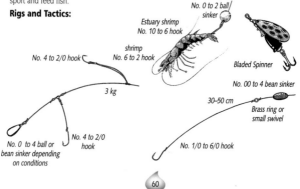

No. 0 to 2 ball sinker

Estuary shrimp
No. 10 to 6 hook

shrimp
No. 6 to 2 hook

No. 4 to 2/0 hook

3 kg

Bladed Spinner

No. 00 to 4 bean sinker

30–50 cm

Brass ring or
small swivel

No. 0 to 4 ball or
bean sinker depending
on conditions

No. 4 to 2/0
hook

No. 1/0 to 6/0 hook

TROUT, BROWN

Scientific name: *Salmo trutta*. Also known as Brownie, sea trout, Loch Leven trout.

Description: The brown trout is a handsome fish which can exhibit wide colour variations, partly dependent upon the environment in which the fish is found. River fish can have a beautiful golden sheen and large black spots on the upper body. There are frequently beautiful red spots, surrounded by a white halo below the lateral line which may be mixed with black spots.

The dorsal fins have some spots but the tail fin has none or a few very faint spots. The tail fin is either square or very slightly indented. The adipose fin is obvious and may be lobe-like in larger fish. The mouth is large and the jaws become hooked to a degree in males during spawning. The brown trout can reach 25 kg overseas, but in WA a fish of 3 kg is exceptional.

Fishing: Brown trout are generally the most highly regarded Australian trout species, due to their large size and the skill which is needed to entice these fish to strike. Brown trout take a variety of foods which may include other trout, minnows, insect larvae, terrestrial insects, snails and worms.

Best times are dawn, dusk and at night.

Many brown trout are taken on fly, with nymphs, streamers, wet flies and dry flies all taking fish. Brown trout generally prefer the slower waters of pools or the tails of pools in streams, moving into feeding stations during peak periods. Brown trout are also taken on a wide variety of lures, with favourites including lead head jigs, spoons, bladed lures like the Celta, and minnow or yabby lures. Brown trout take a variety of baits, with mudeyes, yabbies, minnows, grubs and worms being most successful. Brown trout are found in only a few waters in WA and are much prized.

Rigs and Tactics:

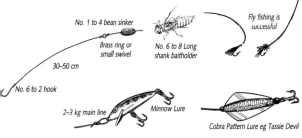

TROUT, RAINBOW

Scientific name: *Oncorhynchus mykiss.* (*formerly Salmo gairdnerii*) Also known as rainbow, 'bow, Steelhead.

Description: Rainbow trout possess the fleshy adipose fin of all salmonids behind the dorsal fin. The tail may be slightly forked but characteristically rainbow trout have spots over the entire tail and all of the body except the belly. A pink stripe along the body ranges from very pale in sea run and lake fish to crimson in river fish and those on their spawning run. Male rainbows develop a hooked lower jaw as spawning approaches. Females retain a more rounded head. Many WA fish have many heavy spots.

Fishing: Rainbow trout are generally easier to catch than brown trout but usually fight harder and often jump spectacularly. Rainbow trout are more mobile and will feed more freely in mid to shallow depths.

Rainbow trout prefer faster water in streams and will take up station in riffles in WA. Rainbow trout can be taken on fly, lure or bait. They take dry flies, wets, nymphs and streamer flies. Rainbow trout can be taken on bright colours and gaudy streamer flies can work well. Rainbow trout take all baits. A lightly weighted worm in streams or fairly close to the bank takes fish as do mudeyes fished under a bubble float.

Rigs and Tactics:

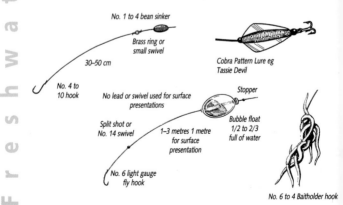

No. 1 to 4 bean sinker

Brass ring or small swivel

30–50 cm

No. 4 to 10 hook

Cobra Pattern Lure eg Tassie Devil

No lead or swivel used for surface presentations

Split shot or No. 14 swivel

1–3 metres 1 metre for surface presentation

Stopper

Bubble float 1/2 to 2/3 full of water

No. 6 light gauge fly hook

No. 6 to 4 Baitholder hook